Contents

ACKNOWLEDGMENT

This book is the end product of my being surrounded by an amazing family, friends, and colleagues.

However, I give all thanks, glory, and honour to God for giving me the privilege to learn, write and pass this knowledge on to generations.

This book would have been impossible without the support and motivation of my loving husband Akin Odunlami and our adorable son Simi Odunlami. Akin stood by me all through my career transition and kept me motivated in my lowest of lows and I am indeed grateful. Words cannot explain my appreciation.

To my amazing parents; Femi and Adeola Fajolu, my siblings; Gbemi Olofin and Tomi Fajolu, my darling friend Ayo Taiwo, thank you all for believing in me irrespective of the fact that you had no clue on Scrum, you supported me all through this journey.

Further appreciation goes to my boss, mentor, coach, and friend, Phil Awbery-Maskell for believing and constantly encouraging me in being a better Scrum Master.

And finally, to everyone who believed in me, thank you all and God bless.

INTRODUCTION

D ear Scrum, thank you for finding me, or should I say, thank you for letting me find you. It is indeed an intriguing journey.

On Becoming Scrum is highly beneficial for newbies to Agile methodology using Scrum or to curious individuals who just seek to be enlightened as to what this term is.

I mean let's be frank, the first time we heard the word Scrum we probably chuckled, wondered what in the world this word meant or for the fast fingers; simply embarked on a Google search.

Most books I have read about Scrum give the basics with regards to the roles, events, rules, and artifacts without a detailed process of how one with no prior IT background can become a Scrum Master.

The silent norm is that to succeed in the role of a Scrum Master, you either have to come from an IT discipline as a software developer, business analyst, tester or project manager but guess what, I became a Scrum Master without coming from neither of the above disciplines. However, I did go through the process of consistency, perseverance, and dedication.

In no way do I disregard books or journals that go straight to the Scrum rudiments, as most of these books have been instrumental towards the preparation of my certification exams and my current role. However, as humans, we love real-life experiences which of course are relatable.

In the next couple of pages, you will see a detailed experience with illustrations on how I have made Scrum work for me and my organisation.

How you decide to process this book is totally up to the reader. The reader can opt to dive into a chapter that seems more beneficial in terms of solving a specific need or might decide to simply start from Chapter 1. Whichever method of progression is adopted is well acceptable. No matter what chapter you begin with, On Becoming Scrum is guaranteed to add optimal value to you

So, let's dive right in

CHAPTER 1

IN THE BEGINNING

T he two founding fathers of Scrum are Jeff Sutherland and Ken Schwaber. However, Scrum product development was first coined in 1986 Harvard Business Review by Hirotaka Takeuchi and Ikujiro Nonaka

In 1993, Sutherland created the first Scrum project, and in 1995, Sutherland and Schwaber developed Scrum as a formal process at the OOPSLA (Object-Oriented Programming, Systems, Languages, and Applications) conference and in 2001 along with 15 other software development leaders converged at a ski resort in Utah which led to the creation of the Agile Manifesto for Agile Software Development and the Principles behind the Agile Manifesto

Manifesto For Agile Software Development

- Individuals and interactions over processes and tools

- Working software over comprehensive documentation

- Customer collaboration over contract negotiation

- Responding to change over following a plan

12 Principles Behind The Agile Manifesto

- Our highest priority is to satisfy the customer through early and continuous delivery of valuable software.

- Welcome changing requirements, even late in development. Agile processes harness change for the customer's competitive advantage.

- Deliver working software frequently, from a couple of weeks to a couple of months, with a preference to the shorter timescale.

- Business people and developers must work together daily throughout the project.

- Build projects around motivated individuals. Give them the environment and support they need, and trust them to get the job done.

- The most efficient and effective method of conveying information to and within a development team is face-to-face conversation.

- Working software is the primary measure of progress.

- Agile processes promote sustainable development. The

sponsors, developers, and users should be able to maintain a constant pace indefinitely.

•   Continuous attention to technical excellence and good design enhances agility.

•   Simplicity--the art of maximizing the amount of work not done--is essential.

•   The best architectures, requirements, and designs emerge from self-organizing teams.

•   At regular intervals, the team reflects on how to become more effective then tunes and adjusts its behavior accordingly.

Scrum On

Scrum is one of the Agile frameworks and according to the Scrum Guide; Scrum is a framework for developing, delivering, and sustaining complex products. So maybe you are wondering what Agile is, well in simple terms, Agile is the umbrella for Scrum.

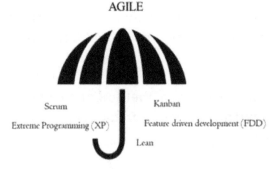

In a more thorough definition, Agile is a process used for managing and controlling iterative and incremental projects where demands and solutions evolve through the collaborative effort of a self-organizing and cross-functional team.

Increments V Iterations

Increments are tasks accomplished in a step by step sequence while

Iteration, on the other hand, is done in cycles.

ILLUSTRATION

Imagine you were saving for a mortgage on your current monthly salary. On the 25th of each month, you receive £1000 and save £100.

This is an iteration because the same amount is saved on the same day of the month hence it becomes a cycle.

On the other hand, say at the end of 6 months we can save £600 towards our mortgage; this is an increment.

This is in all reality is the scrum practice. Iterations in scrum are called sprints carried out within a week to four weeks cycle while the delivery a potentially shippable item or product is an increment

Agile can indeed be practiced in different ways and Scrum is one of many. Asides Scrum, other approaches include Lean, Kanban, Feature Driven Development (FDD), Xtreme Programming amongst others but let's stick to Scrum here since that's what we intend to become.

In a nutshell, Scrum is an incremental and iterative agile product development framework that ensures that the highest value is delivered to the consumer or customer in a time-box. The time-box which is known as a sprint is usually within a week to a maximum of four weeks.

Essence Of Scrum

a)   Project Transparency and Visibility

As opposed to a traditional methodology where teams go away for a while to work on their respective tasks, Scrum brings everyone together and ensures the steps to delivering a project is as transparent and visible to each member of the team.

Scrum is aware that different individuals interpret differently hence the usefulness of Scrum.

We are all aware of the popular nursery rhyme Mary had a little lamb. Let us imagine we had never heard this rhyme and we asked a group of individuals to interpret this sing-along you'd be shocked what this innocent rhyme might interpret.

It could mean:

Mary ate a little lamb either for lunch or dinner

Mary gave birth to a little lamb

Mary had a little lamb as a pet (the original interpretation)

Mary had a little lamb that is now dead

Forgive me if I have scared the meaning of this rhyme but you get the idea. With Scrum, it helps remove all the uncertainties.

b)   Enhance quality

With Scrum, the end product oozes quality as the team can fail fast and improve its standards through each sprint by properly inspecting and ensuring products match the desired end product.

c)   Manage changes to projects, Speed to market

Changes are easier to manage in a scrum project as the framework gives room for this. With transparency and a clear understanding of what the project entails, impediments are removed along with the early delivery of.

The Dating Website Project

To understand the concept of a traditional methodology and an agile project using scrum, we will be using the illustration of creating a dating website.

A group of businessmen decides the dating market is flourishing and they would like to invest in this industry. At the moment, they have a team of developers, project managers, business analysts, and testers and would like to launch this product at the earliest possible time so they can begin to yield profit.

So let's begin the project using the traditional approach popularly called the waterfall methodology and in Chapter 2, go through the delivery same project using scrum.

Illustration Of A Waterfall Project

With our dating website project, we have a requirement gathering phase where the business users and customers tell a development team what they want, how they want it and when they want the product delivered.

We then have a business analyst or project manager coming up with heavy documentation and a strict timeline as to when this site ought to be delivered. So, in this case, we give this project six months' timeline.

After 5 months, coding is done and then it is time for the team to test if their codes work and meet the business requirements.

Boom! Most of the codes are broken, 5 months of hard work with little or no result and then the developers begin to fix bugs. Remember we have a six months' timeline where we want a fancy dating site we promised our business users and stakeholders. The developers then start to fix the mess in a rush and code sub standardly just to deliver.

On the big release day, the codes work but clearly, the end product looks shabby. Asides the business users not being too impressed with their agreed outcome, their competitors have added a new feature which is a dating app where customers can easily download an app on a smartphone which enables the site to be used on the go.

So yes, that is six months of wasted manpower, effort, funds, and every other expense you can think of. This is enough to demotivate a team.

The Waterfall approach strengths lie in the logic of planning and its weakness in the fact that software is an ever-changing process and businesses evolve hence a strict approach is almost impossible.

Another weakness of the waterfall approach is that it goes through the stages of requirement gathering, design, implementation, verification (also known as testing) and then maintenance. All these stages are great to tick off when working on a project with minimal risk.

With a high-risk project which is far from being predictable, the waterfall approach is rigid with these stages and a team is unable to proceed to the next stage without completing the previous stage.

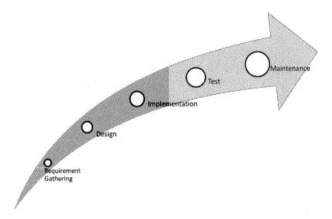

In the next chapter, we will give a detailed breakdown of how scrum works and why our dating website would excel in a scrum environment

How Scrum Works

Scrum is founded on empirical process control theory. In all sincerity, most scrum masters have this empirical process memorized as this question always comes up during certification exams, and I must admit, I did fall into the category of memorizing the scrum process control theory as opposed to understanding it.

Empiricism simply means knowledge that comes only by practically doing something.

The empirical process controls three pillars which are transparency, inspection, and adaptation which helps to optimize predictability and control risk.

For the framework to function; there are set roles, artifacts, events, and rules governing this framework.

Scrum Values

Scrum has 5 values that guide the interaction of people inside and outside of the Scrum team. These values consist of Focus, Openness, Respect, Courage, and Commitment

Focus inherently means members of the Scrum Team should not be side-tracked by doing other work outside of the sprint goal

Openness ensuring the team is candid with how and what the team is doing irrespective of challenges faced.

Respect everyone is to be respectful and respected while ensuring individual knowledge is valued.

Courage The team can overcome challenges of the work or people outside the team

Commitment The whole team is committed to pursuing the sprint goal

Scrum Roles

There are three major roles for scrum to work: Product Owner, Scrum Master, and Development team. Pretty straight forward if you ask me.

Product Owner

The product owner creates a product vision which may be a document of what the product should do. The PO also creates supporting documents called the project road map. The PO ensures whatever projects being worked on are of business value to the organisation as a whole ensuring a maximum return on investment. A product owner is the voice of the business. The management of the items to be worked on by the team is prioritized in the product backlog. The product owner ensures the product backlog is visible, transparent and clear to all.

The Development Team

When we speak of the Development Team in Scrum, this does not only consist of front and back end developers. It consists of everyone working on an actual project. Depending on the organisation, development teams comprise of testers, UX designers, security analyst, business analyst, programmers, service desk, technical support, software architects, DevOps amongst others

A significant team number should be between 3-9 dedicated members with the appropriate skills required for the project. As opposed to the traditional method, scrum teams do not require any outside interference to function. This is to say, there are no titles or managers within a scrum development team. A manager might, however, be a member of a scrum team but has no authority within this team.

The team is cross-functional with the skilled members required to create a product increment. The team is also encountered and empowered to self-manage and not be micromanaged.

Scrum Master

The most misunderstood role within Scrum framework is that of a Scrum Master. The role is not a project management role he is the opposite- a servant leader.

The Scrum Master does everything to ensure the team is successful in practicing Scrum. The Scrum Master, however, manages the practice of Scrum. The Scrum team manages itself while the Product owner manages the business goal and vision.

ILLUSTRATION

Imagine a sheep and a shepherd. The shepherd will do everything in its power to prevent the wolves from disrupting the sheep and ensures the sheep are led to safety. That's exactly what a Scrum

Master is, a shepherd. Not a manager, but again, a servant leader.

The Scrum Master also coaches the organisation as a whole on Scrum and how the organisation can help the team achieve its goals.

The Scrum Master also works with the Product Owner by ensuring the project vision is understood by all, ensuring the Product Owner arranges the product backlog to maximum value and facilitating scrum events as requested.

The Scrum Master cannot be the Product Owner as this is a conflict of interest and will disrupt the purpose of scrum and its deliverables

In summary, a Scrum Master renders services to the development team, the product owner and the organisation

Sprint Events

SPRINT PLANNING

The task performed in a sprint is planned for during the sprint planning. The time-box for a month sprint is 8 hours and shorter sprints are usually shorter. In sprint planning, the team selects the highest priority task into the Sprint Backlog.

There are usually two phases during sprint planning which consists of what the product vision and goals are how the product will be developed in terms of slicing user stories into actionable task

The Sprint

Product developments are done in cycles (also known as iterations) which are called sprints. Sprints are typically time-boxed to a maximum of one week to one month. Each sprint has a goal of delivering a potentially shippable item towards the product vision.

Sprints may be cancelled before the time box is over only if the sprint goal becomes obsolete. A Sprint goal being obsolete occurs in a circumstance where the company direction has changed or if there is the emergence of a new technology.

Sprint Goal

The Sprint Goal according to Scrum Guide guides the Development Team in why it is building the increment. The Sprint Goal should, however, be determined by the Product Owner at the start of the sprint planning and then reviewed by both the Development Team and Product Owner at the end of the sprint planning meeting.

DAILY SCRUM

This is a 15 minutes time-boxed event irrespective of the size of the development team. This event should be done at the same time and venue for consistency. The Daily Scrum is by no means a status report me instead, it is a meeting for the team to inspect and collaborate on the task.

Three proposed questions are said to be answered during a Daily Scrum:

What I did yesterday to help the team towards its Sprint Goal

What I am doing today towards the Sprint Goal

What impedes (blocks) me from completing my task in this Sprint

SPRINT REVIEW

The Sprint Review is usually done at the end of the sprint. This event is usually a four-hour meeting for a month sprint and shorter for shorter sprints.

This is where the Scrum team (Product Owner, Development Team and Scrum Master) and Key Stakeholders (invited by the Product Owner) inspect what was done during the Sprint.

SPRINT RETROSPECTIVE

This event usually takes place right after the Sprint Review for the team to inspect itself, performance, processes and plan towards improvements for subsequent Sprints. A one month sprint will usually have three hours retrospective and shorter for shorter sprints

PRODUCT BACKLOG REFINEMENT

This is not listed as one of the events in scrum, but the backlog refinement popularly called backlog grooming is a key event that should take place before the beginning of a new sprint.

According to the Scrum Guide, backlog refinement should consume no more than 10% of the Development team's capacity.

The refinement session aims to ensure the team has a basic understanding of what is in the product backlog and if possible estimate. By doing this, it avoids a situation of the team being clueless during sprint planning.

This session does not require the attendance of all the team and attendees can be shuffled as appropriate. The PO is, however, a compulsory attendee

Scrum Artifacts

Product Backlog

This is a living document managed solely by the Product Owner. The Product Backlog comprises all that is needed to ensure the product vision comes into reality. Product backlogs are usually written in user stories.

User stories are short descriptions of the feature told from the perspective of the user. A user story usually consists of the user, benefit, and feature to be produced.

Example

As a user, I want to log into the website so I can view my dashboard.

Please be aware that nowhere in the Scrum Guide does it state that every backlog must be written in user stories. They are just simple to understand and interpret and most organizations have adopted this.

Sprint Backlog

This is more of a subset of the product backlog. The Sprint backlog is more like a shopping list of products you want to produce in the sprint. It contains just the things the team would work on during the sprint. The Development team manage the sprint backlog as the team is self-organizing

Increments

This is a sum of items completed in the current and the previously completed sprint. Increments are used for transparency so the Scrum Team can determine uncompleted and completed tasks during the sprint and measure it alongside the product vision. Increments are usually delivered by the Development team.

Burndown Chart

The burndown chart is not a scrum artifact. According to Scrum Guide; it is, however, a useful graphical representation that depicts the task remaining in a sprint done versus the work yet to be completed.

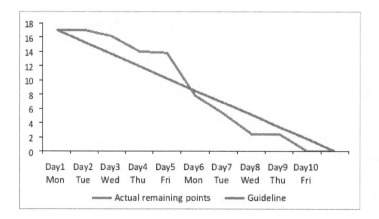

The positives about this chart is its visibility to every member of the Scrum team as it gives a quick indicator of the progress of the project and helps to identify and deal with issues early before they become a problem.

Definition Of Done

The definition of done is an elusive term when it comes to individual tasks as opposed to a collective task formulated by all members of the Scrum team. In Scrum, everyone on the Scrum Team needs to agree with and understand what done means during a Sprint.

A developer done with coding is an illustration of a wrong definition of done. Coding might be done but does not mean the code has passed the testing phase and we all know the number of bugs that might be discovered while testing so in real terms, the developer is far from done.

If a development organisation has a set of guidelines or policies this is, however, the minimum definition of done. If this is inexistent, the scrum team should, however, develop what the definition of done is. The definition of done is by no means an increment

The definition of done varies across the organisation, risk and skill set of the scrum team.

Here is an example of a Scrum team's Definition of Done:

a)   Coded to standards

b)   Peer reviewed

c)   Unit test passed

d)   Deployed to test environment (Feature passes regression testing/smoke test)

e)   Acceptance criteria, functional and non-functional requirements

f)   Feature is documented (tasks in the user stories are completed)

g)   MVP or potentially shippable product

h)   Feature ok-ed by Product Owner

The Dating Website Project

Remember the dating website we spoke on using the Waterfall

methodology in Chapter 1? Having gone through in detail the essentials of practicing Scrum, we can analyze why Scrum fits the delivery of our fancy site.

Using a two weeks sprint time box, the team can fail fast with inspection and quickly adapt new changes even when competitors come up with a new feature like the dating application.

At the end of each sprint, the scrum team is able to come up with a functional or potentially shippable dating site which might not in any form be the desired end product but a site where the business users and key stakeholders can review the teams work, make suggestions, add or remove features with respect to their desired vision and market.

CHAPTER 2
MY JOURNEY

My first degree was in Mass Communication, with a Master's in Business and Management in view. About work experience, I have taken up a varied amount of roles ranging from Sales Consultant, Business development analyst (non-technical) and a Data Analyst. There was not an ounce of IT in my background asides the basic computer skills. On the other hand, my husband, a Lead Software developer inhales and exhales IT. I did want a career change but had no inkling as to what this change was going to be.

Of course, he did want me to switch careers to his field and he proposed two courses: Business Analysis and Project Management. I opted for Business Analysis and I got reading immediately.

Moving forward, I will refer to my husband as my career adviser as I am sure there'd be a lot of eye rolls with the frequency in which I use the term my husband and this is of no means a love story. However, he does play a significant role in where I am today.

One major helper was the fact that I love to read. I was highly inquisitive so I dug into every BA book and article there was. I read for the British Computer Society foundation exam and passed. Following this success, everything became quiet. I forgot about everything BA and no, I didn't lose interest; I guess family life and my current role as a Data Analyst took preference.

My career adviser who was in the loop of all my career development then suggested I go read about Scrum and sent some helpful videos. On completion of those videos, my heart and eyes instantly lit up; literally. I loved what I read irrespective of the fact that I had no clue with regards to the practicality.

I instantly booked for the certified Scrum Master course with no fear of failing. I read day and night, and at that time, my first child was 15 months with me being tired most nights from chasing him around, juggling work and cleaning up the house. Notwithstanding here is where the passion came in. No matter how tired I was, I always found a way to read.

The Birthday Present

At the time, as a female in my late 20's, the last thing I wanted to do was seat for an exam on my birthday. To my surprise, when I booked this date, I was oblivious to the date of my exam till it crossed my mind that I was born on a certain day which was fast approaching.

In all humility, with the way I read and prepared towards this, failing was not an option. I scored all marks right and that made a perfect birthday present. And that's how I became a Certified Scrum Master.

Reality Of A Certified Scrum Master

There is this saying I have heard several times and I say this with no mincing of words. Does the certification give you the qualification of being a Scrum Master? Professionally, YES. Practically, NO

In my honest opinion, one is a Scrum Master with experience. Being certified is an icing on a cake as Scrum is indeed light-weight, simple to understand but difficult to master

With all that I had read, I was not practically ready for this discipline. My first couple of interviews were a mess as I was so nervous.

In Chapter 6, we will look through all the interview questions I was asked throughout my journey of becoming a Scrum Master. And if you are wondering how I can remember all my interview questions, I jotted them down after each interview. Fortunately, most Scrum Master Interview questions are repetitive so that's a positive.

I had some pretty good interviews where I thought I nailed it and I would wait for 20-30days only to get an, unfortunately, I have not been shortlisted feedback.

So I decided to go back into a familiar field which was Data Analysis and Sales Consulting and to my utmost surprise, all the interviews attended within this field thought I was too qualified for their roles.

And I gave up. Yes, I did.

I stopped applying, starting eating, caught up with the latest television series, took my son to every playgroup close to the house and I just decided to live my life outside Scrum and outside transiting to a different career. It was so bad to the extent of ignoring recruitment agent calls as one could easily tell their numbers. I was done with false hope. What dampened my spirit, even more, was the fact that I had already visualized myself writing this book since I passed my certification exam and the only way I could begin was to start a role in this discipline.

Fortunately for me, there was an opening for a Scrum Master and Business Analyst role at a start-up which I was shortlisted for. I got to work with both front end and back end developers and I finally had the opportunity to put into practice all the months of reading.

In addition to this amazing opportunity, I given a JIRA and Confluence account which are one of the major tools used by IT teams in most industries.

And again, I began to read! Indeed I had landed into the career of my heart desires but reading made me current and by being current; I was able to introduce modern-day practices. Knowledge is power and in reality, there is no knowledge lost in reading.

My passion for agile and scrum began to take over me as I watched videos, attended seminars, collaborated with other scrum masters and put in the best I could with regards to the team dynamics and transparency of task

Reminder, never go into a field you aren't passionate about, it will tell in your output

Moving on...

In about a month within this role, I was very confident as I wrote user stories, acceptance criteria and held all the scrum meetings. I was indeed grateful.

The next chapter would go into more granular details of my first couple of days as a Scrum Master but as a Scrum Master just like every role, you go through a learning phase because what you read in the books is very different from what happens in reality.

Common Errors Of A Scrum Master

Most aspiring and already Scrum Masters make similar errors concerning how the Scrum events are held. From experience, I will ensure a detailed breakdown of common errors I have made in the past, and errors I have witnessed from other scrum teams.

The Do Not List

Sprint Planning

During the sprint planning session here are common mistakes the Scrum Master should stay clear of;

a)   The Scrum Master should not own the conversation during this session.

The sprint planning is for two reasons; for the product, owner to discuss the business vision and the business needs while the second session is for the team to tackle and breakdown the stories brought forward by the PO with actionable task. In either session, the sprint goal can be determined.

b)   The Scrum Master should not outline or assign a task to the team members.

The team decide what task their skill set can deliver as they are to be self- organized

Sprint

a)   Do not have a sprint for more than one month.

An organisation might have been working on a '7weeks sprint' before your joining the team and as a Scrum Master, you are the scrum expert. In order words, guide them far from this practice.

b)   Do not give room to team members who work on a task outside the sprint.

When members of a scrum team are working on tasks outside the ongoing sprint and are not accounted for, then what is the purpose of the sprint? Agreed there are emergency change requests which should be accounted for by the Scrum Team.

c)   Do not accommodate hardening practice

This is pointless. So here is an example, a team has a 3 weeks sprint and decides the first two weeks are to investigate stories and clear technical debts and then the last week is when there is an adrenaline rush to complete this sprint. What happened to sprint refinement which is used to understand the stories before the sprint? What happened to a 1-day spike used to investigate the stories? Stay clear from a hardening practice

d)   Do not accommodate sprint zero

The refinement session handles the need for a sprint zero and no-where in the scrum is guide sprint 0 an event.

Daily Stand-up

a)   The Scrum Master should not allow the development team to be seated

This beats me. It is in the name Daily Stand-up. A scrum master should be strict and not for once allow a team member to be seated unless that individual has some medical exemption. Stand-ups are to be quick and on the spot

b)   The Scrum Master should not allow this meeting exceed it's 15 minutes time-box

On a personal note, I am not able to stand for more than 20minutes at a stretch. I will get dizzy and probably fall. Once the scrum team seems to be taking longer to discuss on a task, then a separate meeting should be held outside the stand-up to further discuss this task. Also if the team is done with this event in 5 minutes then they do not require being in the room for 10 extra minutes to fill in the time.

c)   The Scrum master should ensure the daily scrum is not a status report

A status report is mundane and usually does not involve collaboration which is the opposite of what Scrum is trying to achieve

d)   The team should not be addressing the Scrum Master

The daily scrum is for the team to collaborate and be transparent on the tasks they are working on and if they might need some additional assistance from another teammate. When it looks like the team is reporting updates to the Scrum Master then this is more like the traditional project manager route. Once the team is mature, the Scrum Master should let the team facilitate and co-ordinate their stand-ups while ensuring it is time-boxed.

Sprint Review

Do not ignore this event even if no stakeholders have been invited

Agreed that the PO and the stakeholders are in this event are meant to review and then propose their inputs towards the Product Backlog. However, if there is no new functionality this demo does not occur but the team should, however, review each task.

Do not go into a review without preparation

Stakeholders ask questions, and as a scrum master, you should be conversant with the teams' work.

Sprint Retrospective

a)   Do not go into a retrospective without an agenda for the meeting.

This is the last thing you want to do as you do not want to seem disorganized for

b)   Do not drop the sprint retrospective

Some teams drop the retrospective thinking it is a waste of time; this is quite the opposite.

The team usually come together to work on the sprint and a good retrospective can help the team bond

c)   Do not accept for a team member to permanently opt-out of a retrospective

Some team members do not see the benefit of a retrospective and they believe it is a waste of time. However, this is a wrong conception. Every single member should be present asides for when they are on holiday or sick leave; asides that, the sprint retrospective takes precedence as the intent is to improve the team.

Conclusion

In conclusion, as a Scrum Master, you are also an accurate time-keeper. Do not go late for any of the events. If you as a Scrum Master cannot be bothered to be on time then the team owe it to no one to be timely.

All meetings especially the sprint retrospective should work towards a positive approach and tangible outcome.

SCRUM EVENTS AGENDA

The title Scrum Master means you are the company's scrum expert and a lot of dependencies fall on you if the organisation is transitioning into scrum.

I have had the opportunity to create scrum event agenda as a guide for all the roles and outside stakeholders who feel there is a need for them to be in attendance of all scrum events.

Below is a sample agenda for all scrum events

Sprint Planning

The sprint planning is an event for establishing immediate goals and identifying requirements. This event is usually split into two stages: *What and How.*

The *What* stage is where the Product owner addresses the team with prioritized business needs while the *How* stage is where the Development team works on how to deliver the requirement

Required Attendees

- Product Owner

- Scrum Master

- Development Team

Optional Attendees

- Field Experts

WHAT STAGE

Agenda Item

- Situation Overview: product vision, roadmap
- Sprint Goal
- Defining the highest priority and acceptance criteria

HOW STAGE

Agenda Item

- Brainstorming And Slicing: discuss the solution, slice user stories into actionable tasks, team member's commitment to tasks, and discover spikes

- Story Points Estimation: determining story complexity using Planning Poker

- Sprint Capacity: how much can the team undertake in terms of compiled story points, holidays, training, and company events

- Sprint Goal Review: finalize on the sprint goal after stories have been sliced and estimated, ensuring the desired outcome is clear among all team members

- Task Boards: ensure the waste snake and burndown charts are set up to capture the sprint

- Definition Of Done

- Define what each team member is tasked with

- Address any issues noted throughout the meeting

Daily Scrum

This optimizes team collaboration and performance by daily inspecting the work and forecasting upcoming Sprint work

Required Attendees

- Development Team

Optional Attendees

- Product Owner

- Scrum Master

SAMPLE AGENDA

In the daily stand up event, the development team can discuss and update task board around the below sample questions

What did I do yesterday that helped the Development Team meet the Sprint Goal?

What will I do today to help the Development Team meet the Sprint Goal?

Do I see any impediment that prevents me or the Development Team from meeting the Sprint Goal?

Sprint Review

This event is held at the end of the Sprint to inspect the Increment and adapt the Product Backlog if needed.

Required Attendees

- Product Owner

- Scrum Master

- Development Team

- Key Stakeholders (invited by the Product Owner)

Optional Attendees

- Customers

AGENDA

- Introductions: The Product Owner introduces everyone in the meeting room, highlight the agenda for the review

- Sprint Assessment: Recap sprint goals, product items included in the sprint, explain the business value of each feature and why it was prioritized

- Live Demonstration: The Development Team reveals the new features and functionalities explained from the user's point of view

- Risks and impediments identified in the sprint, organisational level impediment are highlighted along with a proposal for solutions

- Feedback: questions and answers   from the stakeholders

Sprint Retrospective

The sprint retrospective is an opportunity for the development team to inspect itself and create a plan for improvements to be enacted during the next Sprint.

Required Attendees

- Development Team

- Scrum Master

Optional Attendees

- Product Owner

SAMPLE ACTIVITIES

- Analyse the Waste Snake
- What went well, What could be improved, What should we try next
- Liked, Learned, Lacked, Longed For
- Strengths, Weakness, Opportunities and Threats
- And lots more ...

Conclusion

The above are sample agendas as to how each scrum event should hold. Teams are welcome to adopt this approach, modify or simply use a different method without omitting the three pillars of scrum which are transparency, inspection, and adaptation.

CHAPTER 3
FIRST 30 DAYS AS A SCRUM MASTER

I am indeed excited about this chapter as I have looked forward to sharing this experience way before I became a practical and certified scrum master.

For individuals with no prior scrum master experience, this could be indeed daunting especially when you do not want to look like a counterfeit Scrum Master.

I have been a Scrum Master at two different organizations with different business visons. However, the first couple of days in both were very similar.

Day 1

Unlike my previous roles where I got scheduled into training, this was nothing like that. Do not get me wrong, I did get trained on the business however I was not trained on how to do my job because a Scrum Master is more of a senior role and or a management role depending on the organization.

So on this day, I got introduced to the IT team and no, I was in no form nervous. I mean with all the reading, certifications and preparation, I just wanted to dive in.

I had a brief company overview with my line manager and by brief, you possibly cannot take it all in one day hence my business knowledge was more of continuous learning as I progressed.

I got my system and mobile phone set up with an induction plan sent in by HR.

As of all the first days, I got to go home early.

Day 2

Scheduled a meeting to meet with the Product Owner and then got scheduled into a JIRA process review to understand how the company as a whole wanted to manage tickets and if they were going about it the right way.

I jotted questions down for the Product Owner because irrespective of how much of a good memory you have, looking unprepared for a meeting is the last thing you want to portray whether or not you are new to the company.

Having prepared ahead of my meetings, I found myself getting lost in the office building as with me, I do not properly integrate until I am faced with finding my way around my new office

Day 3

It was a productive meeting with the PO as we spoke about our personal lives and touched base on where the company is and where they want to be. Your PO and Scrum Master needs to have a good working relationship else your Scrum Team is in trouble if otherwise.

The very first company I was a Scrum Master in wanted a JIRA overview created as a guide to the users. Ironically the second organisation I scrummed for wanted similar however, this guide served seven different scrum teams.

Again, my first couple of days for both organisations were similar; however, for the next couple of days, I will be more specific on my experience with the second organization.

Day 4

The role of a Scrum Master is mainly that of coaching, mentoring and facilitating. On this day, I met again with the PO and my agile coach (also my line manager). This meeting was more of a strategy on how to make scrum work, coach and ensure the team was carried along every step of this transition.

After this, my manager wanted me to give a brief training to the Telecoms and Service Desk teams to carry everyone along on the IT floor with regards to the New Way of Working (NWOW). I must admit I was nervous not because I had to come up with slides as I think coming up with slides amplifies my imagination; I was because I had no clue as to if they were for or against this NWOW.

On speaking to both team managers, they were ready for my Scrum Overview the next day! It was a Thursday and I figured they'd want to have this meeting on a Monday which would have given me more time to prepare, I was however very wrong. So here I am, in the middle of the day having to come up with a Scrum slide which again I loved but needed to ensure the right words were picked for the presentation.

Day 5

As luck would have it, one team cancelled and wanted the scrum overview the following week which put me in a better place.

The other team was amazing! Receptive, asked questions and again as luck would have it, a team member was well aware of the scrum process.

So that's my first week as a Scrum Master.

Day 6

On my 6th day, I went through the Scrum Overview with the team that cancelled a week before. By this time, I had built up my confidence and it was more of a breeze.

I also had to work on the JIRA guide so I had another meeting with the senior business analyst and my manager on a couple of suggestions made before my resumption which I had to factor into my guide.

Day 7

This was a rather quiet day as I had no meeting. On this day, I decided to read up as I have always done and research on new methods to optimize teams before their first sprint

Day 8- 9

I was booked in for a 2 days user story workshop that lasted the whole day with different project managers. This for me was an avenue to further understand the business and the problems that needed to be solved.

I must confess I do not think I have ever spent this much time writing and analyzing user stories alongside acceptance criteria's

Day 10

Day 10 for me was used to recover from the two days' workshop as my hands were wobbling from all the user stories written. The user story workshops were indeed very productive.

I met with the Scrum Masters of the other teams as you would recall, there were 7 scrum teams. The meeting was to understand where they were in the Scrum journey and to share and collaborate on knowledge.

Day 11

I had completed the JIRA guide for the scrum teams and presented to my manager and senior business analyst who made the necessary adjustments

Day 12

I spent the day fine-tuning the JIRA guide as I was to present this document to the IT Leadership team. This was another level of presentation. I wanted it perfect, I wanted to be audible, and I wanted my ideas to be properly passed so I gave this document my all.

Day 13

This was indeed the D day to present my proposed JIRA guide.

When nervous, I have my ears turn red and they sure we're on the heat on this day.

My nerves eased towards the middle of the meeting as I felt more comfortable and confident; after all, they weren't wolves.

The IT Leadership team asked questions and made suggestions to the document and they were a pretty lively group of individuals.

Day 14

The organization as a whole launched the New Way of Working which was transitioning to Scrum and this was yet another whole day's event

Day 15- Day 20

As the Jira guide had been officially released following the implementation of ideas of the IT Leadership team, I started training
the organization as a whole. And my confidence level was pretty
high at this stage. I knew my cookies, had gotten over my nerves
and I loved it.

Pretty much carried out sessions across scrum teams, scrum
masters and anyone else who was interested in knowing about
this tool.

Day 21

Asides the Jira guide training, I had decided to come up with a retrospective tool kit to help the other Scrum Masters and the organization as a whole as we were currently in the transition stage.

I loved this document and I will share some sprint retrospective techniques to help all current or upcoming scrum masters.

Day 22

The retrospective tool kit kept me very busy as I wanted the Scrum Masters' opinions before the start of the first sprint.

Day 23

I had a catch-up with the PO and we discussed having an agenda for all the scrum activities. With this document, roles are clearly defined with details regarding duration and clearly defining each scrum member's role.

Day 24

Very busy day for me indeed as I intended to complete the retro-spective tool kit and the scrum meeting agenda document.

Ended the day as planned and scheduled a meeting with the IT leadership team to review these documents

Day 25

I utilized the morning to know my slides inside out and went through a practice presentation as I do before any meeting. The meeting was to hold towards the close of business so I had time to coach a bit.

The leadership team loved the agenda and with their request, a glossary was added to the document as an aide to individuals not too familiar with scrum terminologies.

Day 26

Given the fact that I was a scrum master to two teams and was filling in for my boss who was on holiday, I had inherited an additional team making me a scrum master of three teams for the time being.

On this day I had sprint planning sessions for two of the teams which indeed took most of my day.

With a fantastic PO who already had the items in the backlog prioritized, the team had something handy to work with.

I adopted the planning poker game for story points and to my utmost surprise; I had one of the teams not so keen to participate in the game. After explaining the benefit and each member having their story points matching twice in a row, these got them loving it.

Day 27

As I had facilitated two sprint planning sessions a day before, I had two daily stand-ups. I loved the team as they were all excited with the NWOW and collaborating with how they tackled the tasks in the current sprint.

I felt some sort of self-fulfilment.

I spent the other half of my day on my third team's sprint planning. Compared to the previous two, this team had more individuals with a lot of dominant personalities. This is not to say the other teams were naïve, the members of those teams had worked together making it an easy transition.

The session did go surprisingly well and this was the end of another fulfilled day.

Day 28

I now had three stand-ups I was a part of and I decided to create a virtual burn down chat on Microsoft Excel for the team to give them visibility of their progress. I also set up a virtual progress board for two out of the three teams as the last team preferred using the digital boards.

I implemented a Waste Snake during the sprint planning sessions which is technically used to capture items not included in a current sprint. We would discuss the Waste Snake in detail in subsequent chapters.

Day 29

The daily stand up for one of the teams was a bit flat maybe because the team members were new to Scrum so I introduced the Bull (Ruby ball) which served as a talking token

A lot of Scrum Masters during daily stands ask individual team members for status on their assigned task. For me, I was well aware that this was not a status report meeting; instead, it was more of a transparent and collaborative 15 minutes meeting to inspect and adapt progress to the sprint goal.

Given that the teams were new to agile, I started the daily scrum by asking the team member's for their task updates which meant calling on them to answer the 3 questions in the stand-ups and then after a week, once they understood the drill, I introduced the bull which is to be passed across the team and anyone with the bull addresses the team on the task they are working on in the current sprint.

As a scrum master, work with whatever works for the team; so far they are following the scrum rules then you are fine.

Day 30

On Becoming Scrum is a seed of my passion and imagination with the scrum framework so, on this day, I began to write.

So that's it. 30 days as a Scrum Master. If I could handle it, so can you.

CHAPTER 4
STORY POINT ESTIMATION

This is by far the most debatable topic there is about Scrum. And this is because Scrum teams try so hard to implement what they have read or learned from previous organizations.

Keep it simple and do not over complicate things. Scrum is hard to master and there is a lot of learning especially when new teams implement this. The whole point of Scrum is to fail fast.

Estimation can be done using t-shirt sizing: small, medium, large or x-large, MOSCOW, Finger Voting, Fibonacci sequence: 1, 2, 3,5,8,13,21 and any other technique that works for the team.

Some scrum teams decide on estimating stories in days while other estimate story points to complexity. There is no wrong or right way prescribed by scrum as scrum does say teams should estimate but how this is done is dependent on the team. These are only estimates, not promises.

My insight on this is to have fun with estimations.

I have worked in organisations where the team members have never worked together hence they have no velocity or baseline to determine estimates. They simply used the Fibonacci sequence to factor in the complexity of the task and after 4 sprints, they were able to determine their velocity and the number of hours or days a 1, 2, 3 or 5 story point meant.

Some teams, on the other hand, have worked together, and have decided to look through previous projects done as a guide to how large an 8 pointer is.

Others decide to use a t-shirt sizing approach and match them with the Fibonacci numbers.

Whichever the case may be with regards to estimation, ensure the team as a whole is in collaboration with how estimations are done.

Tactics For Handling Disruptions And Delays In Sprints

Hard truth, but let's face it things do not always go as planned in a sprint. Scrum Masters want everything within the sprint to go as intended; sprint planning with the team chucking in task they can complete within the time duration, no disruptions from senior management or key stakeholders, no unplanned sick leaves, absolutely nothing to disrupt an ongoing sprint. Well, unfortunately, the exact opposite happens. This not the fault of any scrum member, in particular, it just happens to fall within the forming and storming stage of any scrum team.

The good news is, it can be managed with the right skills, personnel, and experience. As a guide to how to manage unplanned work in a sprint, a list of 'The 6 Acts' has been compiled to help teams adjust to an ever-changing environment

The Act Of Trading Stories

Every organization has stakeholders who want it all. Unfortunately, this mind-set leaves many scrum teams demotivated from over-committing.

In a situation where this arises with the proposed task requiring a lot of effort, a trade by barter should occur.

The Product Owner should inform stakeholders when their demands are unrealistic and instead of adding this on to an already started sprint, replace the less urgent task on the sprint with the new one. It is a give or take circumstance.

The Scrum Master, on the other hand, should protect the team ensuring there are no burned out team members.

Example

In the second week of a sprint, a stakeholder wants a new feature to be added to a website that most competitors are using which now takes precedence of some task in the current sprint. The Product Owner after the approval of the Development Team then trades a task of the same size in the already started sprint to fit in the new feature. Simple!

The Act Of Absorbing

There might be some tasks that the development team can absorb as it could be as simple as a text change. However, neither the PO nor SM should add this task to a current sprint without prior confirmation from the Development Team.

It is fair that only the Development Team decides what can be absorbed as they determine how the work is done.

Example

A stakeholder noticed a spelling error in recently deployed software and wants the text to be changed. In reality, this task takes about 3 minutes to fix if all goes as planned. The team agrees to absorb this with an already started sprint without a grave impact to the sprint scope

The Act Improve Prioritizing

The backlog refinement is an exercise where the tasks are properly prioritized, valued and estimated. Most scrum teams pay little or no attention to backlog refinement which will at some point draw the team back.

The scrum guide recommended teams to give no more than 10% of their time to backlog refinement. The reason being is the product backlog would not be new to the development team during sprint planning which saves time and also, the PO can refine the tasks in the appropriate priority and if need be get back to the stakeholders to set correct expectations about delivery.

The Act Of Boosting Quality

In most cases, the frequency of a site being broken is determined by the quality of work completed by the development team. If the development team produces a shabby code, a shabby end product shall be received leading to a constant demand for fixes.

To avoid this, teams are advised to pair program which means a developer writes code and another developer looks over it to avoid errors and mistakes. Another practice that can be introduced is Continuous Integration and delivery (deployment) which automates software and avoids human errors.

Example

In a situation where the stakeholder's sprint after sprint keeps disrupting the team with regards to bugs in features released. If these were one-off it is possibly something the development team can absorb; however, if this is constant then the quality needs to be improved. With time the stakeholders would lose trust in the team which is even more of a greater issue.

The Act Of Negotiation

In some circumstances, there might be no stakeholder interferences which is amazing; however, the development team might not be able to deliver the agreed task on the backlog and would need to resolve to negotiate with the Product Owner in terms of splitting up the task and carrying over to the next sprint.

In my opinion, I'd rather the development team split task, focus on that which can be done and carry over to the next sprint as oppose to not completing any task

The Act Of Saying No

This is by far the most precise act of all. Most scrum teams forget this word exist which would do the team a whole lot of good if they learned to say no to interruptions mid-sprint.

Having said this, the Product Owner is to be firm and influential explaining to stakeholders how the team can only seldom handle urgent tasks. By doing these it saves both the development team and scrum master time to focus on the current sprint.

CHAPTER 5

RETROSPECTIVE TOOL KIT

R etrospective ought to be fun, lively and useful for the team's future progression. A good scrum master should ensure this event is active and action points are taken into consideration.

This chapter would give you tips on several exercises that can spice up your team's retrospective and enable each member to reflect in terms of steps on improving subsequent sprints.

Most teams follow the basic retrospective activities of what went well, what did not and what can be improved. Which is not in itself bad but again basic which means the teams will get bored after some time?

Here are is a brief retrospective tool kit with procedures on conducting these activities. To get more retrospective exercises, Agile Retrospective Making Good Teams Great by Esther Derby and Diana Larsen is an amazing go-to book for more tips and insight.

The Waste Snake

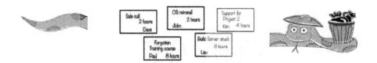

Source: Simone Vicentini https://www.purplebeans.co.uk/the-waste-snake/

The snake is meant to capture all events which disrupted or altered the teams focus from an ongoing sprint hence the name 'waste snake'

To get this snake effective, this should be implemented at the start of the sprint and placed the team room or wherever is easily accessible to the team. The goal of this living object is to tackle how to reduce activities done outside an ongoing sprint and monitor if there is a trend.

At the end of the sprint during the retrospective, the waste snake should be analysed factoring the number of hours spent doing on sprint work.

This activity is usually time-boxed at 5-15 minutes to analyze depending on the size of the team and the amount of waste.

STEPS

- Every time a team member gets interrupted within a sprint, he/she writes the details and the time spent on a sticky note

- The team member then adds the note to the waste snake on the wall

OUTCOME

- The team gets a visual interpretation of all unplanned task

- It is also a really good way to find out if there are repetitive tasks that continuously interrupt the team during iterations.

- Actions to take to reduce the content of the waste snake.

Safety Gradient Chart

I particularly love the safety gradient chart as this can be used to collect data for teams who experience conflict. Another to like about this chart is its ease of use; and is time-boxed roughly 5-10 minutes depending on the team size and participation is completely anonymous.

Smith S (2006), Crosstalk: The Journal of Defence Software Engineering was where the safety check gradient chart was first published. The purpose of this exercise is to ensure people feel safe to share their ideas.

Level	Description	Comment
4	Secure	Everything is discussable without filtering
3	Safe	Almost everything is discussable without filtering
2	Neutral	Most things are discussable without filtering
1	Dangerous	Many of my best ideas are not discussable
0	Treacherous	Most of my best ideas are not discussable

STEPS

- Sticky notes are distributed to the development team

- Anonymously they fill it with the number that matches how safe they feel

- Each member places it into a hat, ballot box, or anything that can act as a container

- The facilitator or any other team member compiles and interprets the data

Level	Description	Number of People
4	Secure	XXXXX XXXXX (10)
3	Safe	X (1)
2	Neutral	XXXX (4)
1	Dangerous	XXXX (4)
0	Treacherous	(0)

The above is an example of complied data and the aim of this exercise is to get everyone feeling safe and secure to voice their opinions.

If you have most of the team feeling in a dangerous or treacherous environment, then you have an issue and this should be worked on immediately.

Teamwork Chart

After a couple of sprints, the facilitator or the scrum master needs to review how the team feels about the level of team work.

The steps are very similar to the safety check gradient.

How satisfied are you about teamwork?

1.   We are the best team on the planet

2.   I am glad to be a part of this team and how we work together

3.   I am fairly satisfied; we work well together most of the time

4.   I have some moments of satisfaction

5.   I am unhappy and dissatisfied with the level of teamwork

The interpretation of the data is similar to the safety gradient chart

Oscar Academy Awards

This activity takes sprint retrospective to another different level. It encourages the team to be involved in tasks well enough to rate which tasks fall into the categories of best tasks, most annoying task, and most exciting tasks.

The Oscar Academy identifies achievements and enables the team to discuss in detail on specific events that took place in completing the tasks and methods of improvement. It is learning.

Most importantly, if your organization writes tasks in user stories, it triggers conversations towards identifying the criteria of a well-written user story that the team is confident in delivering

This activity is time-boxed to 20-45minutes depending on the team size and how many tasks were worked in the sprint.

STEPS

- First, explain the game to the team and clarify any outstanding questions

- Draw a 3 parts starfish on a flip chart sheet. Write down the 3 categories: best tasks, most annoying task, and most exciting tasks.

- Write down the user stories of the past Sprint on post-its or alternatively, project the Sprint Backlog out of the tool you use (Jira, Monday, etc.) because the team will be able to open user stories as needed to remember its description, tasks, and notes

- Give the team 5minutes to identify what stories fall into that category

- Give the team 10 minutes to nominate User Stories in each category. This part is collaborative and generates conversations

- Identify the top user story in each category by dot voting

- Facilitate a discussion with the team about why the

selected stories are the best in their respective categories.

Liked, Learned, Lacked, Longed For

This activity is as simple and straightforward as the title. Throughout a sprint, each team member would have encountered activities within the sprint that either put them off or encouraged them, and the sprint retrospective is an amazing avenue to sorting these emotions out.

STEPS

- First, explain the game to the team and clarify any outstanding questions

- Divide a flip chart into 4 parts writing each category: liked, learned, lacked and longed for.

- Give the team about 5-8minutes to think about what to include in each category

- Team then has 5 minutes to write and place post-it notes in the appropriate category

- Speak through each category and dot vote to prioritize the order of importance

CHAPTER 6

INTERVIEWS AND CAREER PROGRESSION FOR A SCRUM MASTER

I hate to blow the trumpet of On Becoming Scrum but this is yet another very beneficial chapter. I wish I had a compilation of interviews with real-life examples as oppose to textbook examples because organizations that are already practicing Agile can spot a newbie in a couple of seconds.

On the flip side, a newbie Scrum Master might be lucky if he is being interviewed by an organization that is just about to transition or aren't even sure they want to practice Scrum full on.

Whichever the case might be, here are some of the most popular interview questions with real-life examples.

Heads Up

These interview questions and answers are in no way intended to be used to falsify your qualifications, knowledge or experience. These are guides and if you are a Scrum Master or becoming one, using these exact examples to answer interview questions would not work for you because as the saying goes, you need to have practiced what you preach.

So in no order of importance let's begin

a)   What might be a possible reason if a team's performance velocity is constantly falling?

Many factors affect a team's velocity;

The movements or shuffle of individuals within a team will reduce a team's velocity which is a short term reduction in productivity but this is temporal as the new team member picks up with time which will eventually improve velocity

Level of seniority; when you have a manager in a scrum team with his subordinates in the same team, most of the time you find his subordinates taking directives with regards to the task from their manager instead of the prioritized tasks on the Product Backlog. This is, however, a bottleneck which is why scrum states there are no titles in the team

Holiday or sick leave, without proper refinement, I have noticed that the scrum teams plan for work when they are on holiday and concerning circumstances beyond the Scrum Masters reach, team members might call in sick leaving their task undone

When the definition of done is inexistent; usually the definition of done is a guide for the team to know when the user stories are completed if this is not properly stated, it could adversely affect the team's velocity

b)   What is an indicator that agile is working?

From my experience, you notice the team's velocity increases steadily which is usually followed by improved team happiness

c)   What is the difference between Agile and Scrum?

Scrum is a subset of Agile. Agile is a broad spectrum while Scrum is a form of Agile. Other subsets of Agile include XP, Kanban, and Lean amongst others.

d)   How do you introduce Scrum to Senior Executives?

For scrum to be successful in any organization, the senior executives need to be in tune and see the value of going agile. Once senior executives are on board, subordinates usually follow suit. From my experience, I have been in organisations where the Senior Executives were the initiators of scrum so the knowledge of scrum was in the air. On the other hand, I have been in an organization where I had to introduce this framework which leads to holding 2-3 days' workshop sessions depending on their schedules and tackling any fear and anxiety they have. I once had a workshop where an attendee wanted the team's velocity to increase each sprint which is a common misconception. My advice was simple; team A might have a velocity of 5 while team B might have a velocity of 12. This in no way means team B is performing better, as projects vary in size, risk, skills, and so many other factors

e)   Difference between the iterative process and the increment process?

Increments are done stages or steps while iterations are done in cycles (Refer to Chapter 1)

f)   What is an empirical process?

Empirical process simply refers to the act of knowing things through practice.

g)   How do story points work?

Story points are used to determine the complexity of a user story or task. Most of the time especially if the project is a new one, the team is unable to give a defined time estimate to the duration required in completing each story; hence the use of story points to estimate each task.

Over time, once the team has built some sort of familiarity around the project, the team can give rough estimates as to how long a task will take. Story points are in most organizations I have been with an estimate using the Fibonacci sequence.

h)   What type of estimates do you know?

Estimation can be done using various techniques which include T-shirt sizing, planning poker, finger counting amongst others.

i)   What is your favourite retrospective technique and why?

Refer to Chapter 6 and speak on your favourite choice

j)   How do you handle conflict?

Conflicts within teams are inevitable. However, from my experience, the best strategy is not taking sides and aim to be objective. From experience, I have witnessed an environment where the test and development team never see eye to eye with regards to the user stories and requirements.

Noticing this, I simply directed them to the business analyst who is in charge of the initial requirement gathering and ensured at least a member of both teams is present at the refinement meeting which significantly reduced the reoccurrence of this.

k)   Explain Scrum

Refer to Chapter 1

l)   Difference between Scrum and Kanban?

Refer to Chapter 1

m)   How do you handle remote workers?

Irrespective of the fact that it is highly beneficial for organizations to have co-located teams, in some organizations this is close to impossible.

Luckily for us, the emergence of collaborative tools has helped close this gap. Tools like slack can be used for communication and tools like Jira and Monday can be used for task transparency and collaboration.

With regards to meeting times and stand-ups, and where you have teams in different time zones, each member should be able to reach a concession and if possible take a rota on the activities around this.

n)   How do you ensure multiple projects do not clash and teams are not doing the same thing?

This is as a result of the benefit of having one product backlog. With one product backlog irrespective of the existence of multiple teams, a single product backlog gives visibility to everyone on which tasks are picked up and by what team.

Also, holding regular scrum of scrum meetings is a helpful event as this drives conversation around what the individual scrum team is working on.

o)   What are the main skills of a Scrum Master

They are Servant leadership, communication, facilitation, conflict resolution, and time management.

p)   How do you handle a stakeholder requesting for a change in a current sprint

That's a job for the Product Owner hence the reason for having a firm product owner. However, in some circumstances, the requirement might be urgent like a broken website, in this case, if the team can absorb this extra task without affecting the sprint or its goal, all well and good.

If this would affect the delivery of some items on the sprint, then the business would have to lose something on that sprint to gain another which in this case is the fixing of the site.

q)   How do you motivate a team?

Teams have different personalities that can be handled if they are properly motivated. From experience, individuals generally do not like to be macro managed so I stay clear from this. I also give recognition when tasks are completed. By doing this it motivates team members to work hard and be on top of their task.

Also, depending on the company budget, taking the team out is a great motivation technique

r)   What is a spike?

A spike is a task that cannot be estimated as the Development Team might have no in-depth knowledge on the task hence a short investigation is carried out to determine the complexity of the task.

Scrum In A Nutshell

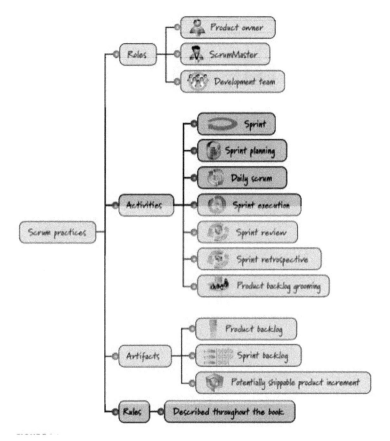

Source: Rubin K.S (2012:14): Essential Scrum

THE END